INTRODUCTION

Why would anyone invent a flying bedstead?
Believe it or
not, this device
was designed to test
whether jet aircraft could
take off straight upward and hover in midair.
From it, came a world-class combat
aircraft: the jump jet.
Many inventions begin as something strange
and are designed and redesigned, tested and
retested, before the final version is achieved.
Very few are made by one person, alone and
overnight. The process can take years and
usually involves lots of people and lots of money.
There are dozens of fascinating facts in this book.
You can test what you've read—and some of what
you may already know—with the Young Observer trivia
quiz at the end of each chapter.
If you get stuck, the answers
are in the back.

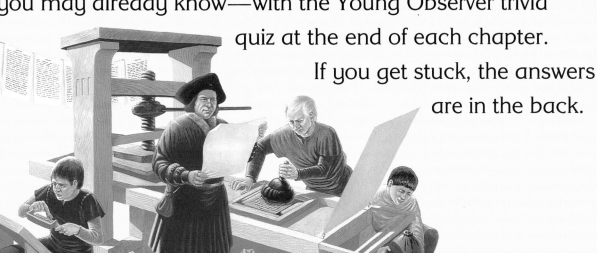

CHAPTER ONE

GETTING OUT AND ABOUT

Once upon a time, people had to walk—everywhere. There were no planes, trains, boats, or cars, not even carts or chariots. You used your own two legs.

Fokker triplane fighter (World War I)

People first took to the water, messing around in boats and canoes, thousands of years ago. Back on land, we discovered our helpful four-legged friends, horses and oxen. But it was the invention of the wheel that began the transportation revolution...

THE FIRST BOATS were floating logs or bundles of reeds, or even animal skins blown up like balloons—you sat on, paddled with your hands...and fell off! Dugout canoes date back more than 20,000 years. By 5,000 years ago, Egyptian boats had masts with sails and were steered with oars. Frenchman Claude d'Abbans built the first ship with an engine. This early steamboat puffed along the Saône River in 1783.

By the 1830s, some ships had paddle-wheels, while others had screw propellers. Which was best? In 1837 the British Navy set up a tug-of-war between the Alecto *with paddles and the* Rattler *with screws.* Rattler *won, and screw propellers took over.*

Screw propeller

Paddle wheel

YOUNG OBSERVER
THE FLYING BEDSTEAD
and other ingenious inventions

Steve Parker

Kingfisher

NEW YORK

KINGFISHER
Larousse Kingfisher Chambers Inc.
95 Madison Avenue
New York, New York 10016

First American edition 1995
10 9 8 7 6 5 4 3 2 1
Text copyright Larousse plc 1995
Illustrations copyright ©
  Larousse plc 1995
Design copyright © David West
  Children's Books 1995

LIBRARY OF CONGRESS CATALOGING-IN-
PUBLICATION DATA
Parker, Steve.
The flying bedstead and other
ingenious inventions / Steve Parker.
—1st American ed.
p. cm.—(Young observer)
Includes bibliographical references
and index.
1. Inventions—History—Juvenile
literature. [1. Inventions—History.]
I. Title. II. Series.
T15.P36 1995
609—dc20 95-6107 CIP AC

ISBN 1-85697-574-6

Printed in Hong Kong

Conceived and created by

David West • CHILDREN'S BOOKS

Consultant: Ian Graham
Cover illustrations: Ian Thompson
  and Rob Shone
Illustrations: Alex Pang 4–5, 6–7,
  8–9m & br, 10–11, 12t,br, 13b,
  14tl, 15mr, 16–17b & r, 18–19tr &
  m, 32r & mr, 33m, 35br, 36bl &
  br; Ian Thompson 8tl & ml, 9t & r,
  12–13m, 14–15b, 16l &m, 20–21,
  24–25, 28–29, 30, 32tl, 33br, 34b,
  36t, 37r & br; Mike Saunders 18bl,
  19br, 22tr, 23tl, tr & br, 24bl, 26tl,
  bl & tr, 27tr & br, 32ml, 34tl & tr,
  35tl & tr, 36mr, 37tl; Rob Shone
  22b, 26–27m; Eric T. Budge 8bl
Line illustrations: Rob Shone

CONTENTS

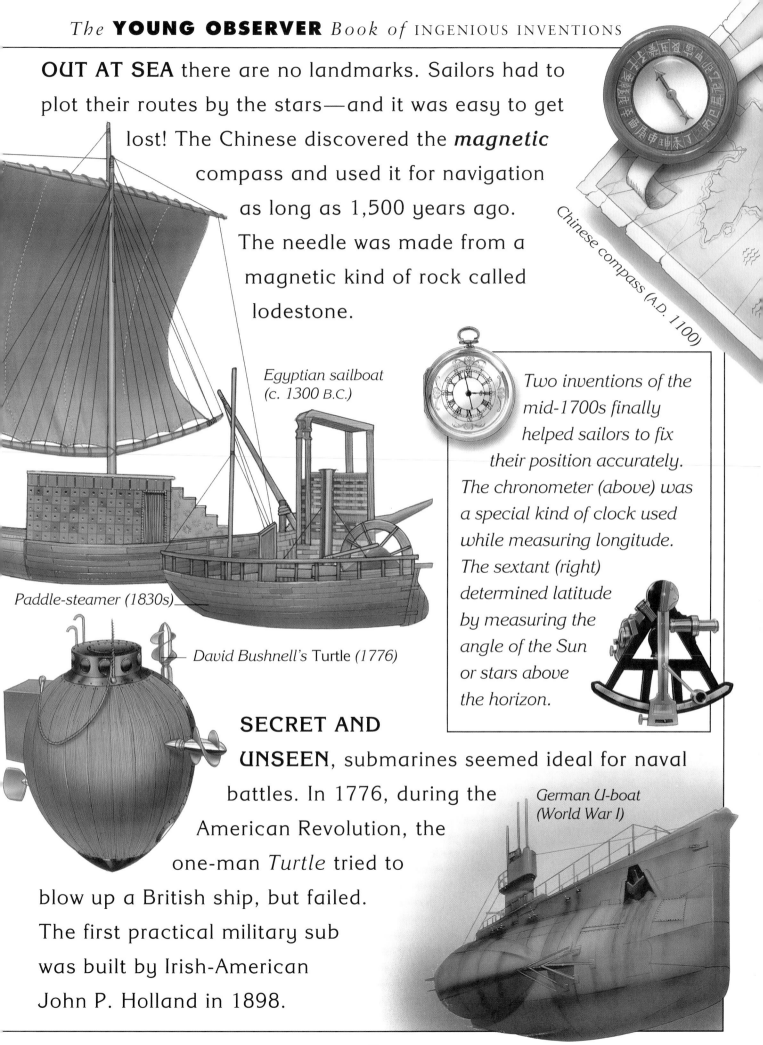

OUT AT SEA there are no landmarks. Sailors had to plot their routes by the stars—and it was easy to get lost! The Chinese discovered the *magnetic* compass and used it for navigation as long as 1,500 years ago. The needle was made from a magnetic kind of rock called lodestone.

Chinese compass (A.D. 1100)

Egyptian sailboat (c. 1300 B.C.)

Two inventions of the mid-1700s finally helped sailors to fix their position accurately. The chronometer (above) was a special kind of clock used while measuring longitude. The sextant (right) determined latitude by measuring the angle of the Sun or stars above the horizon.

Paddle-steamer (1830s)

David Bushnell's Turtle *(1776)*

SECRET AND UNSEEN, submarines seemed ideal for naval battles. In 1776, during the American Revolution, the one-man *Turtle* tried to blow up a British ship, but failed. The first practical military sub was built by Irish-American John P. Holland in 1898.

German U-boat (World War I)

5

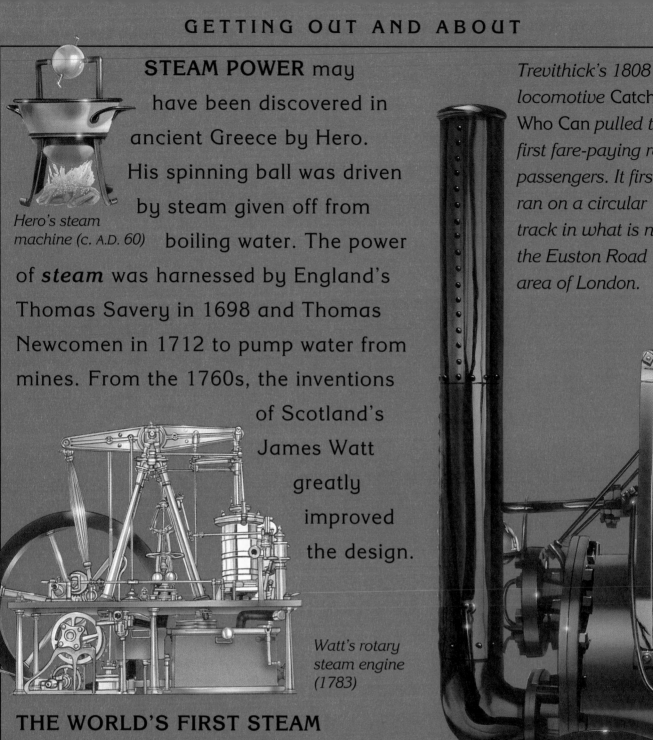

STEAM POWER may have been discovered in ancient Greece by Hero. His spinning ball was driven by steam given off from boiling water. The power of *steam* was harnessed by England's Thomas Savery in 1698 and Thomas Newcomen in 1712 to pump water from mines. From the 1760s, the inventions of Scotland's James Watt greatly improved the design.

Hero's steam machine (c. A.D. 60)

Trevithick's 1808 locomotive Catch Me Who Can *pulled the first fare-paying rail passengers. It first ran on a circular track in what is now the Euston Road area of London.*

Watt's rotary steam engine (1783)

THE WORLD'S FIRST STEAM RAILROAD LOCOMOTIVE was built in 1804 by Cornish engineer Richard Trevithick. The first public steam

Stephenson's Rocket *(1829)*

railroad, the Stockton and Darlington line, opened 21 years later—Englishman George Stephenson built his *Locomotion* for it.

In 1829, Stephenson's *Rocket* set a record speed of 30 miles per hour (without carriages)— finally we could travel faster than horses!

From the 1860s, railroads opened up the American West.

Monorails run on one rail. The first one intended for regular passenger services was built in Pennsylvania in 1872. Its steam locomotive "sat" over the track like a saddle.

ELECTRIC TRAINS had to wait for the invention of powerful *electric motors* in the 1860s. The first ran at an exhibition in Berlin in 1879. The year after, an electric train collected clean clothes for a French laundry company—no sooty smoke!

THE FIRST WHEEL was laid on its side more than 8,000 years ago—the potter's wheel was invented in the Middle East. By 5,000 years ago, in the same region, the Sumerians had turned wheels upright to make horse-drawn war chariots. In Europe, from the mid-1400s, passengers were paying to ride in omnibuses.

Horse-drawn omnibus (1660s)

THE BICYCLE was invented in France in the 1790s. You made the *célérifère* move by pushing your feet along the ground—no steering or

Macmillan's swing-pedal bicycle (1839)

pedals! Germany's Baron von Drais came up with a steerable front wheel in 1817. Over in Scotland, Kirkpatrick Macmillan added pedals with cranks to turn the back wheel in 1839. The chain drive didn't arrive until the 1870s.

Benz's patent motorwagen (1885)

8

THE FIRST MOTOR ACCIDENT

happened in France. Nicolas Cugnot built a steam tractor in 1769 to pull cannons

Cugnot's steam tractor (1769)

for the French army, but in 1771 it careered out of control and smashed into a wall. At this time, several other inventors were also trying to come up with a way of using the **steam engine** to replace the horse.

Seventeen years before Daimler's automobile, Frenchman Ernest Michaux put a small steam engine made by Jean Perreaux on the bicycle of his day, the vélocipède. This 1869 vehicle was the first motorcycle.

GERMAN ENGINEERS

Karl Benz and Gottlieb Daimler developed the *motorwagen* in the 1880s. Benz put **gasoline engines** into three-wheeled horse carts. Daimler's four-wheeler of 1886 had a gasoline engine and was the first true automobile.

Many advances in car racing trickle down to ordinary cars.

MOTORING TOOK OFF

from 1890, but only for the rich. Mass-motoring

Ford sold over 15 million Model Ts in 1908–1927.

began in 1908 in the United States after Henry Ford began **mass-producing** his lowcost *Model T*, or *Tin Lizzie*, on his other invention, the assembly line.

WAR KITES were being flown in China 2,000 years ago to light a nighttime battle or to scare or fire-bomb enemies. We had to wait a long time for the next flying machine to be invented, though. The hot-air balloon was made by the Montgolfier brothers of France and flown for the first time in 1783.

Chinese kite

Montgolfier brothers' hot-air balloon (1783)

ADD A PROPELLER and a steam engine to a long balloon, and you have an airship that you can steer. Frenchman Henri Giffard made the first working airship in 1852.

Giffard's airship (1852)

GLIDERS AND HANG-GLIDERS have no engine. They depend on wind and rising warm air to fly. Germany's Otto Lilienthal pioneered scientific glider flight. From 1891, he designed and piloted more than 15 different hang-gliders. Tragically, he was killed in 1896, crash-landing one of his craft.

A Lilienthal hang-glider (1895)

British inventor George Cayley was experimenting with aircraft design in the mid-1800s. In 1849, his kite-glider carried a worried 10-year-old!

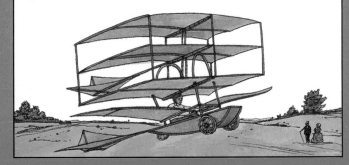

THE WRIGHT BROTHERS were bicycle-makers before they became fascinated by flying machines. In 1903, after four years of tests, they put a gasoline engine and propellers on a glider and made the world's first powered flight. The place was Kitty Hawk, a windy beach in North Carolina. The date was December 17th.

Orville (left) and Wilbur Wright

The wings of Englishman Horatio Phillips' 1907 Multiplane looked like Venetian blinds. Phillips was testing wing shape, but the craft wasn't strong enough, and it collapsed!

Wright brothers' Flyer *(1903)*

Gossamer Albatross *(1979)*

THE DREAM of human-powered flight came true only recently. After centuries of trying to flap wings attached to our arms, we realized that legs are stronger. America's pedal-powered *Gossamer Condor* flew in 1977. In 1979, *Gossamer Albatross* crossed the English Channel between England and France.

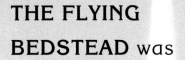

A Whittle test jet engine (1940)

AS WORLD WAR II LOOMED, Britain and Germany were experimenting with a new form of power—the **jet engine**. This sucks in air, sprays it with fuel, and explodes it, blasting out hot gases and thrusting the aircraft forward. Britain's Frank Whittle

Gloster Meteor, first military jet aircraft (1944)

began testing engine designs in 1937. In 1939, Germany's *He 178* was the first jet aircraft to take to the air. It was built by Ernst Heinkel.

THE FLYING BEDSTEAD was designed in Britain, to test vertical take-off. The downward blast from two jets lifted the craft, while the "puffer pipes" at the corners were for maneuvering. Such tests led to the Harrier of the 1960s—this amazing jet takes off and lands vertically, hovers, and flies backward.

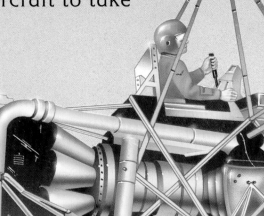

Rolls Royce Flying Bedstead (1953)

*French inventor Paul Cornu built the first rotary-winged craft, or helicopter, to leave the ground. It had two sets of **rotors**, powered by a gasoline engine. In 1907 it chugged to a height of 12 inches, hovering there for just 20 seconds.*

Hawker P.1127 (1960)—early version of the Harrier

ROCKET AND SPACECRAFT

designs were sketched by Russian schoolteacher Konstantin Tsiolkovsky in the early 1900s. They were never built, though—Tsiolkovsky was way ahead of his time! Designed by American Robert Goddard, the first liquid-fuel rocket sputtered skyward on March 16, 1926. The rocket only made it to 40 feet above the ground, but it was a start!

Goddard and his rocket (1926)

ROCKET WEAPONS were developed in Germany in the 1930s, by Wernher von Braun and his team. Their V2 rocket (*right*) was first used in air raids in 1944. After World War II, rocket research continued in the U.S.S.R. and the United States. In 1957, a rocket sent the first artificial *satellite*, Russia's Sputnik 1, into space.

1. V2 warhead
2. Control and guidance systems
3. Liquid fuel tank
4. Liquid oxygen (to burn fuel)
5. Combustion chamber

The first rockets were fireworks that used solid fuel—an early kind of gunpowder called black powder. They were invented in China, where they were being used in warfare by the 1200s—probably for setting enemy camps on fire!

Vostok 1 *(1961)*

HUMANS MADE IT INTO SPACE on April 12, 1961. Russian Yuri Gagarin blasted into orbit in *Vostok 1*, circled the Earth once, and landed again—all in under two hours! Dozens more flights culminated in America's *Apollo 11* Moon landing in 1969, and the first space station, Russia's *Salyut 1*, launched in 1971.

Space shuttle (1981)

THE FIRST REUSABLE SPACE-CRAFT, America's *Columbia* space shuttle,

shot into Earth orbit on April 12, 1981. The first untethered spacewalk took place from *Challenger* on February 7, 1984—thanks to the invention of a jet-propelled backpack —the MMU (manned maneuvering unit).

Space research produces many inventions that find their way into daily life— aluminum foil and non-stick coating for saucepans were both developed in the 1960s for use on American spacecraft. Other inventions include heat-saving silvery blankets for mountaineers, and a super-bouncy rubber used to make toy balls.

An astronaut maneuvers above the Earth in an MMU.

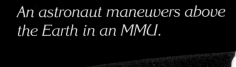

The **Young Observer** *Quiz*

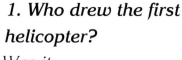

1. Who drew the first helicopter?
Was it:
a) Leonardo da Vinci?
b) Igor Sikorsky?
c) Alexander Bell?

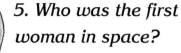

5. Who was the first woman in space?
a) Valentina Tereshkova?
b) Yuri Gagarin?
c) Sally Ride?

2. Which vessel crosses the sea without getting in the water?
Is it the:
a) Hydrofoil?
b) Hovercraft?

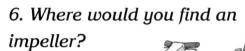

6. Where would you find an impeller?
Is it in a:
a) Jet ski?
b) Automobile?
c) Go-kart?

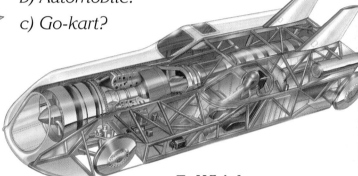

3. Who made a gasoline engine without pistons?
Was it:
a) Rudolf Diesel?
b) Karl Benz?
c) Felix Wankel?

7. Which car was the first to travel faster than 600 mph?
Was it:
a) Blue Flame?
b) Thunderbird?
c) Thrust 2?

4. Who invented the aqualung?
Was it:
a) Jacques Cousteau?
b) Emile Gagnon?
c) David Bushnell?

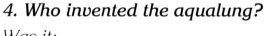

8. Who invented stirrups?
Was it the:
a) Scythians?
b) Mongolians?
c) Chinese?

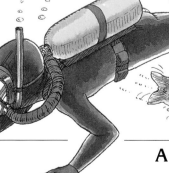

ANSWERS ON PAGES 32–33

CHAPTER TWO

HARD AT WORK

People often invent things to help them do a job or work—there's nothing like sore muscles to get you thinking about making life easier!

Farming inventions began after people started working the land over 10,000 years ago. Many workers moved off the land into factories in the 1700s. Then, in the late 1800s, office work arrived...

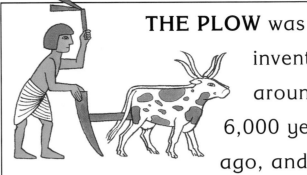

THE PLOW was invented around 6,000 years ago, and at first farmers pulled it themselves! About 3,000 years later, the Egyptians were using oxen to pull their plows. European farmers added a colter to cut the soil, and a moldboard to turn it, over 1,000 years ago.

Moldboard plow (A.D. 600)

SICKLES (*below left*) **AND SCYTHES** were used to harvest crops until the 1820s. Then three people invented reaping machines—Scotland's Patrick Bell (1826), and Americans Obed Hussey and Cyrus McCormick (early 1830s).

McCormick reaper (1834)

Once wheat has been cut, it has to be threshed to separate the grain from the straw and chaff. Today this is done by combine harvesters, but the first threshing machine was made in 1768 by Scotland's Andrew Meikle.

HORSES AND OXEN were kept hard at work pulling farm machines until the 1850s, when steam-powered traction-engines began to give them a rest. The first gasoline-engined tractor was made in the U.S. in the early 1890s, and the *diesel-engined* tractor had arrived by the 1930s.

Modern tractor

Colter

Mold-board

COMBINE ALL HARVESTING JOBS in one machine, and you have a combine harvester (*below*). It reaps, threshes, loads grain onto trailers, and bales leftover straw. American Hyram Moore built the first one in the late 1830s. Harvesters were pulled by animals or tractors at first. By the 1930s, they had their own diesel engines.

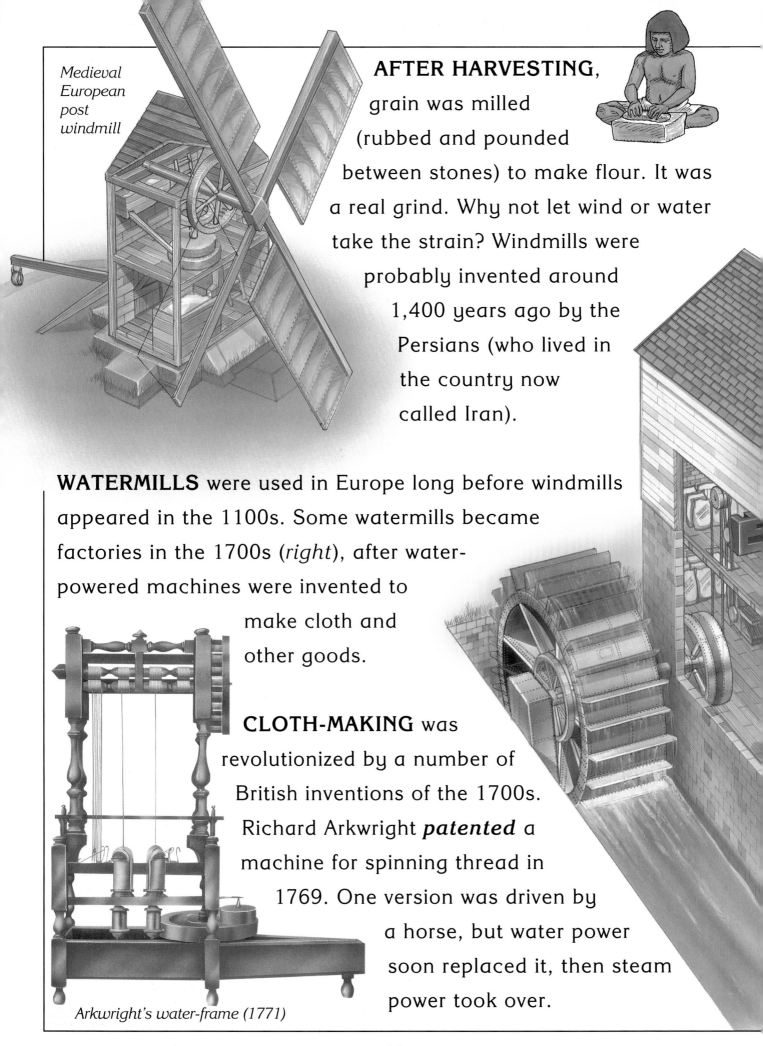

Medieval European post windmill

AFTER HARVESTING, grain was milled (rubbed and pounded between stones) to make flour. It was a real grind. Why not let wind or water take the strain? Windmills were probably invented around 1,400 years ago by the Persians (who lived in the country now called Iran).

WATERMILLS were used in Europe long before windmills appeared in the 1100s. Some watermills became factories in the 1700s (*right*), after water-powered machines were invented to make cloth and other goods.

CLOTH-MAKING was revolutionized by a number of British inventions of the 1700s. Richard Arkwright **patented** a machine for spinning thread in 1769. One version was driven by a horse, but water power soon replaced it, then steam power took over.

Arkwright's water-frame (1771)

18

Arc lamps (1840s)

MODERN FACTORIES

run on electricity. Thomas Edison built the first power station in the city of New York. It used steam-powered **generators**, and on its opening day in 1882 there were only 50 customers wanting to use the electricity!

Briton Michael Faraday's interest in science was sparked off by books read while he was an apprentice bookbinder. Faraday went on to make many discoveries about electricity and to invent the generator in 1831.

THE POWER IN THE

ATOM was released by a controlled **nuclear reaction** in 1942, in Illinois. Italian-born scientist Enrico Fermi and his team built their nuclear reactor in a University of Chicago squash court. In New Mexico, in July 1945, Robert Oppenheimer's team tested the first atomic bomb. The first non-military power station to generate electricity by nuclear reactions opened in Obninsk, U.S.S.R., in 1954.

Obninsk power station (1954)

In August 1945, airplanes dropped two nuclear bombs on Japan.

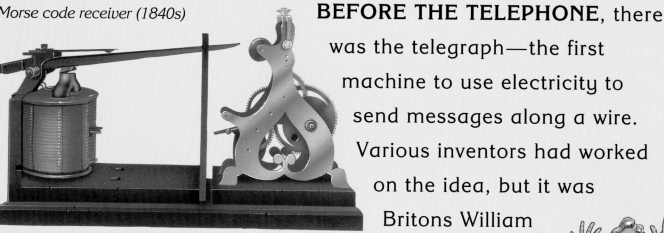

Morse code receiver (1840s)

BEFORE THE TELEPHONE, there was the telegraph—the first machine to use electricity to send messages along a wire. Various inventors had worked on the idea, but it was Britons William Cooke and Charles Wheatstone who patented the telegraph in the 1830s. American Samuel Morse demonstrated his dot-dash Morse code in 1838.

Stick-on stamps, Britain (1840)

COPYING DOCUMENTS and letters was a boring but necessary

Scotland-born American Alexander Graham Bell patented the telephone early in 1876. A few days later, he was working on a prototype when he spilled acid on himself. He called out to his assistant, next door: "Mr. Watson, come here, I want you!" Watson heard Bell's plea over the phone— the first telephone message!

Automatic photocopier (1940)

office chore. In 1938, an American patent lawyer called Chester Carlton invented a xerographic copying machine. But it did not become the standard office photocopier until the 1960s.

British mathematician Charles Babbage invented a mechanical computer in the 1820s, but didn't have the money to complete it. It was finally built in 1991, and it worked!

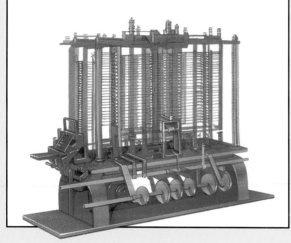

ELECTRONIC COMPUTERS

were developed during the last years of World War II. Alan Turing was part of a British team working on the Colossus series—smart calculators that broke coded German messages. Americans Mauchly and Eckert developed ENIAC—the first real computer. It filled two whole rooms.

Microchip (1971)

Apple II (1978), early personal computer

ROBOTS—machines that take the sting out of hard work by doing it for you—were dreamed up hundreds of years ago. But engineering methods were not good enough to make them until this century. The first robots able to work tools were developed in the 1960s, and from then on computer-controlled robots started to take over some factory jobs. The term robot comes from a Czech word meaning work and was first used in a 1921 play by Karel Capek.

READ ALL ABOUT IT—but it's easier if the message is on lightweight paper and not carved into stone or wood! The ancient Egyptians pulped papyrus reeds into writing sheets 5,000 years ago. But it was the Chinese who mashed and squeezed plant fibers into true paper around 1,900 years ago.

Money can be almost any agreed valuable item, from seashells to bags of salt. Paper money first changed hands in China—it was being printed there over 1,300 years ago.

PRINTING with reusable wooden letters was invented in China about 950 years ago. By the mid-1440s, Johannes Gutenberg of Germany was using a new kind of press and long-lasting metal letters.

Gutenberg printing his first book, the Bible *(1454–1455)*

The **Young Observer** *Quiz*

1. Who invented the milking machine?

Was it:

a) Lee Calvin?

b) Joseph Lister?

c) Louis Pasteur?

2. Where were calculating machines invented?

Was it in:

a) Japan?

b) China?

c) Iraq?

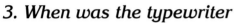

3. When was the typewriter invented?

Was it in:

a) 1768?

b) 1868?

c) 1968?

4. When was the first truly automatic machine invented?

Was it in:

a) 1705?

b) 1805?

c) 1905?

5. What are windmills used for today?

Is it for:

a) Generating electricity?

b) Grinding grain into flour?

c) Pumping water?

6. What did computers use before microchips?

Was it:

a) Crystals?

b) Tubes?

c) Transistors?

7. Who invented the spinning jenny?

Was it:

a) James Hargreaves?

b) Jenny Hargreaves?

c) Jenny Spinner?

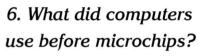

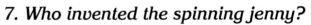

8. Where was the first public hydroelectric power station?

Was it in:

a) England?

b) Norway?

c) Canada?

ANSWERS ON PAGES 34–35

CHAPTER THREE

HOME COMFORTS

As you settle down for an evening listening to music or watching television, think back to the old days. Did people sit in silence, waiting for the radio to be invented, or stare into the corner, hoping for a TV to appear?

Of course not! They could have read a book or played the piano, for a start. But they also had to find time to knead dough, bake bread, preserve food, scrub, sweep, and do loads of other chores—all now done for us by machines!

MOST ACCIDENTS HAPPEN AT HOME, and one of the greatest dangers is fire. So Swede Johan Lunström's safety matches of 1844 lit only when rubbed against the box's special pad.

Shaving was hazardous too, until America's King Gillette invented the safety razor in 1895.

In 1849 another American, Walter Hunt, reinvented the safety pin (first used in ancient Egypt) to pay a $15 debt!

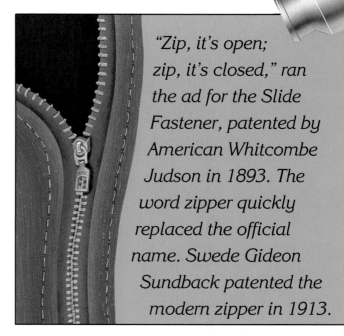

"Zip, it's open; zip, it's closed," ran the ad for the Slide Fastener, patented by American Whitcombe Judson in 1893. The word zipper quickly replaced the official name. Swede Gideon Sundback patented the modern zipper in 1913.

Comb made from deer antler (c. 8000 B.C.)

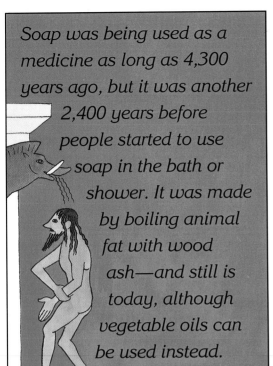
THE FIRST MIRROR was a

smooth pond, long ago in prehistoric times. But by 5,000 years ago, rich Egyptians were gazing into mirrors made of shiny bronze. Combs date back 10,000 years in Scandinavia, but they were probably used for removing ticks, fleas, lice, and other pests, rather than for teasing out the latest hairstyle. Washed hair had to dry in the breeze, until a table-top electric hairdryer arrived in the 1910s, and a hand-held version in 1920.

Electric handheld hairdryer (1925)

Egyptian makeup (c. 3700 B.C.)

Egyptian bronze mirror (c. 3000 B.C.)

BODY PAINTS

have been used since prehistoric times as decoration for ceremonies, war, or hunting. Cosmetics really took off in ancient Egypt—rich men and women lined their eyes with a powder called kohl, painted their lips, and even plucked their eyebrows.

THE FIRST LAUNDRY was done in the river, and clothes were just spread on rocks to dry. The first washing machine was built by American James King in 1851. Clothes, water, and soap were tumbled around inside a hand-turned barrel, then squeezed through a mangle's rollers.

Early washing machine and mangle

Two men invented the electric lightbulb. England's Joseph Swan demonstrated a bulb in 1878. America's Thomas Edison patented his in 1879. They eventually set up a joint company to make bulbs.

ELECTRICITY was wired into homes from the 1880s, mainly for lighting. But inventors soon found dozens of other uses. A vacuum cleaner was patented by Englishman Hubert Booth in 1901. It had a gasoline-powered suction pump with a very long tube—because it was in a truck that parked outside the house! American James Spangler's electric, portable version was made and sold by William Hoover from 1908 onward.

Hoover vacuum cleaner (1908)

Electric kettle, U.S.A. (1891)

COOKS NEEDED STRONG MUSCLES before electric gadgets were invented. Kneading bread dough, whisking cream, and mixing and blending soups and sauces were all very hard on the wrists and arms. An electric whisk went on sale in about 1910, developed from the electric stirrers in milkshake parlors. Mixers with a range of detachable tools were introduced in the 1920s. Then, in 1971, the food processor was invented by Pierre Verdon of France.

Food mixer (1920s)

BREAD WAS BAKED in brick ovens in Roman times, but everything else was cooked over open fires. It wasn't until the early 1800s that people began to install cast-iron, coal- or wood-fired kitchen ranges, with hot plates and ovens, in their homes. Gas stoves became available later in the century, and in 1889 the modern electric oven was invented, in Switzerland.

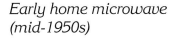

Early home microwave (mid-1950s)

Electric oven (1900)

THE PHONOGRAPH of 1877 was just one of the hundreds of patents taken out by the amazing U.S. inventor Thomas Edison. Sounds were stored as patterns of wavy lines on aluminum foil wrapped around a cylinder. The first clearly recorded words were: "Mary had a little lamb." In 1887, German-born American Emile Berliner introduced a flat, hard rubber gramophone disk, forerunner of the vinyl record. Berliner's disk also stored sound as a wavy groove.

Edison's phonograph (1877)

Berliner's Gram-O-Phone (1888)

VINYL RECORDS

damage easily, and the stylus can wear them away. CDs (compact discs) date from the early 1980s. On these plastic-coated metal disks, sound is stored as a pattern of micro-pits read by *laser* light —virtually wear free.

John Logie Baird's mechanical camera (1926)

Scientists began work on transmitting pictures electrically in the late 1800s. But the first demonstration of television didn't take place until 1926, when Scot John Logie Baird transmitted 15-year-old William Taynton's face. Baird's camera had a mechanical scanner, and it was soon replaced by the electronic scanning TV camera patented by Russian-born American Vladimir Zworykin back in 1923.

ITALIAN GUGLIELMO MARCONI

built the first practical radio equipment in 1895–1896. The system became known as the wireless because radio signals were sent through the air, unlike the telegraph which sent electrical signals along a wire. Public radio broadcasts began in the early 1920s and, in 1954, the Japanese company Sony produced pocket radios, using *transistors* instead of bulky *tubes*.

Marconi's radio transmitter (1895)

Transistor radio (1950s)

IN A TAPE RECORDER,

sounds are recorded as a pattern of tiny magnetic patches, unlike the LP (a wavy groove) or CD (laser-read micro-pits). The first machine, designed by Denmark's Valdemar Poulsen in 1898, recorded sound on a steel wire. Germany's Fritz Pfleumer tried metal-coated tape in 1928. Modern, plastic-based magnetic tapes date from 1935.

Poulsen's Telegraphone wire recorder (1898)

Baird's scanning-disk television (1926)

Early mass-produced tape recorder (1950s)

Sony Walkman, first personal cassette tape player (1979)

THE CAMERA was first described 1,000 years ago—the camera obscura (*right*) was a dark room with a small hole through which light shone, forming an upside-down image of the outside scene. The photographic camera arrived in the 1800s, when people figured out how to use light-sensitive chemicals to record images permanently. Frenchman Nicéphore Niépce took the first photograph in 1827, using a metal plate. American George Eastman began manufacturing the first celluloid roll film in 1889.

Light changes chemicals on photographic plate.

Early camera (1840s)

Lens focuses light rays.

THE MOTION PICTURE was born in Paris on December 28, 1895, when French brothers Louis and Auguste Lumière began using their newly invented camera-projector, the *cinématographe*, to give regular movie shows to paying audiences. Nearly 90 years later, the camcorder (video *cam*era-re*corder*), which uses magnetic tapes and not photographic film, went on sale.

First successful talkie, The Jazz Singer (1927)

WARNER BROS . SUPREME TRIUMPH
AL JOLSON
JAZZ SINGER

Early hand-cranked movie camera (early 1900s)

Camcorder

The **Young Observer** Quiz

1. When was color television invented?

Was it in:

a) 1925?

b) 1946?

c) 1966?

2. When did electric irons first go on sale?

Was it in:

a) 1865?

b) 1885?

c) 1905?

3. How did people start fires before matches?

Did they:

a) Bang stones together?

b) Spin sticks?

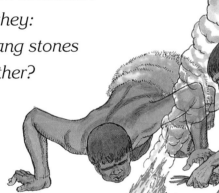

4. When were can openers invented?

Was it in:

a) 1805?

b) 1855?

c) 1895?

5. Who designed the flushing toilet?

Was it:

a) John Harrington

b) Alexander Cumming?

c) Thomas Crapper?

6. Which tailor's workshop was destroyed because he invented the sewing machine?

Was it:

a) Barthélemy Thimonnier?

b) Isaac Singer?

7. Who made the first telescope?

Was it:

a) Galileo Galilei?

b) Hans Lippershey?

c) Anton van Leeuwenhoek?

8. When did lawnmowers replace sheep and scythes?

Was it in:

a) 1730?

b) 1830?

c) 1930?

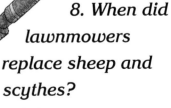

ANSWERS ON PAGES 36–37

The **Answers** to Chapter One (PAGE 15)

1. Who drew the first helicopter?

Answer: a)
The notebooks of the great Italian artist and engineer Leonardo da Vinci (1452–1519) contain designs for hundreds of machines, including a bicycle and a crane, as well as a helicopter with a screwlike rotor. Many of these machines had to wait hundreds of years to be made.

2. Which vessel crosses the sea without getting in the water?

Answer: b)
Hovercraft skim over land or water on a cushion of air. Fans blow air downward, where it is trapped inside a flexible skirt. The hovercraft was designed by Briton Christopher Cockerell in the 1950s and made its test flights in 1959.

3. Who made a gasoline engine without pistons?

Answer: c)
In a gasoline *engine, an air-fuel mixture is lit by a spark plug and the resulting explosion forces a piston down. Changing the up-down motion of pistons into rotary motion to turn the wheels wastes power.*
In the 1950s, German engineer Felix Wankel succeeded in building an engine without up-down pistons—the explosions take place inside chambers, turning rotors around instead.

Air-fuel mixture

Spark plug

Exhaust gases

Piston goes up and down

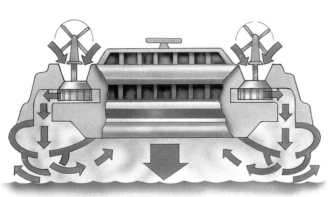

Air-fuel mixture

Exhaust gases

Spark plug

Rotor goes around and around

4. Who invented the aqualung?

Answer: a) and b)
The ancient Greeks were using diving bells over 2,300 years ago, but we couldn't move around freely under water until Frenchmen Cousteau (left) and Gagnon invented the aqualung in 1943.

5. Who was the first woman in space?

Answer: a)

Tereshkova (left) made her 48-orbit flight in the Russian Vostok 6 *craft on June 16–19, 1963. The first American woman in space was Sally Ride, on June 18–24, 1983.*

Thrust 2 *reached 633.4 mph in 1983*

7. Which car was the first to travel faster than 600 mph?

Answer: a)

The rocket-propelled Blue Flame *was the first to travel faster than 600 mph, in 1970.*

Jet engine

Jet cars can go even faster. In 1983, a Rolls Royce aircraft jet engine propelled Thrust 2 *(above) to 633.4 mph.*

6. Where would you find an impeller?

Answer: a)

The jet ski was designed by American Clayton Jacobson in 1963. An impeller works something like a propeller in a pipe, sucking in water and forcing it out backward.

8. Who invented stirrups?

Answer: c)

The Chinese made the first metal stirrups, around 1,700 years ago. Saddles were also first used in this area of Asia by the nomadic peoples who lived in the mountains. But no one is sure who made the very first saddle.

The **Answers** to Chapter Two (PAGE 23)

Jacquard loom (early 1800s)

1. Who invented the milking machine?

Answer: a)

American Lee Calvin invented a way to speed up milking in 1861. He fixed rubber cups over the cow's teats, with pipes leading to the milk bucket. Then he pumped bellows to suck the milk out of the cow's udder.

2. Where were calculating machines invented?

Answer: c)

The abacus began as a board and counters, used for adding and subtracting around 5,000 years ago by the Mesopotamians (who lived in the area now called Iraq). The beads-in-a-frame abacus (above) was used in China about 1,700 years ago.

3. When was the typewriter invented?

Answer: b)

People began trying to make typewriters in the 1700s. The first efficient machine was patented by American Christopher Sholes in 1868 and made by the Remington Arms Company from 1874.

Remington typewriter (1870s)

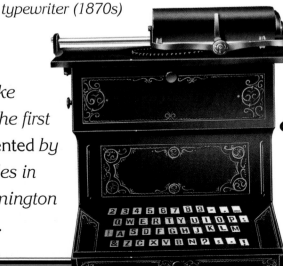

4. When was the first truly automatic machine invented?

Answer: b)

An automatic machine is one that can adjust and run itself, and the first was invented by Joseph-Marie Jacquard of France. It was a loom for weaving patterned silk. Jacquard's 1801 version still took time to set up, and a human operator had to adjust the controls. By 1805, Jacquard was using punched cards with a different pattern of holes for each fabric pattern. This was a truly automatic machine! The idea of punched-card instructions was taken up by Briton Charles Babbage and used to devise a kind of calculator in the 1820s (see page 21).

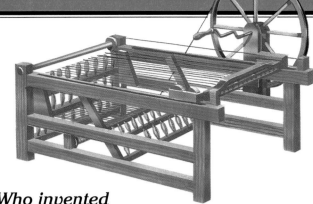

5. What are windmills used for today?

Answer: a), b), and c)
Special windmills called wind turbines are now used to convert the moving energy of wind into electricity. The spinning blades turn a generator which produces electricity. Old-fashioned windmills are still used to grind grain into flour in some countries, or to pump water to drain land.

Generator

Blade

Transistor (1948)

Thermionic tube (1904)

6. What did computers use before microchips?

Answer: b) and c)
Other names for a microchip are silicon chip or integrated circuit (IC). Each tiny IC has the thousands of switches needed to control the flow of electricity and make a computer work. In the 1940s, computers were room-sized because a thermionic tube was used for each switch. In the 1950s, tubes were replaced by smaller transistors, and computers began to shrink.

7. Who invented the spinning jenny?

Answer: a)
Invented by English weaver and carpenter James Hargreaves in about 1764, the jenny was a hand-driven spinning machine which could spin a number of threads at the same time. It was one of several inventions which speeded up cloth-making and led to the mass-production of cloth in factories.

8. Where was the first public hydroelectric power station?

Answer: a)
In hydroelectric power stations, the energy of flowing water is converted into electricity. Water spins a turbine, which spins a generator. The first public station opened in Godalming, England, in 1881, using river water. Large modern power stations utilize the tremendous pressure of dam water.

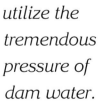

Water in

Generator

Turbine

Water out

The **Answers** to Chapter Three (PAGE 31)

1. When was color television invented?

Answer: a)

Vladimir Zworykin (see page 28) designed a color TV system in 1925, soon after his black-and-white one. But there were many problems, and color TVs did not appear in homes until the 1950s and 1960s. In modern TVs, three guns fire streams of invisible particles called electrons at the screen, making colored dots glow.

Shadow mask

Three electron guns, one each for red, blue, and green dots

Electromagnets direct electrons toward screen

Electrons sweep across screen to build up picture

2. When did electric irons first go on sale?

Answer: b)

Simple flat irons, heated on a fire, have been around for centuries. American Henry Seely produced an electric iron in 1882, and it went on sale in 1885.

3. How did people start fires before matches?

Mouthpiece

Answer: a) and b)

Prehistoric peoples discovered that banging stones such as flint together produces sparks that will set alight tinder (dry grass or leaves). They also could make fire by friction: pulling a bowstring made the tip of a stick spin until it was hot enough to light tinder in a hollow in another stick.

Bowstring

Tinder

4. When were can openers invented?

Answer: b)

When food was first canned in the early 1800s, people used a hammer and chisel to open the cans! It wasn't until 1855 that the claw-lever opener made the job easier.

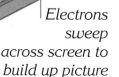

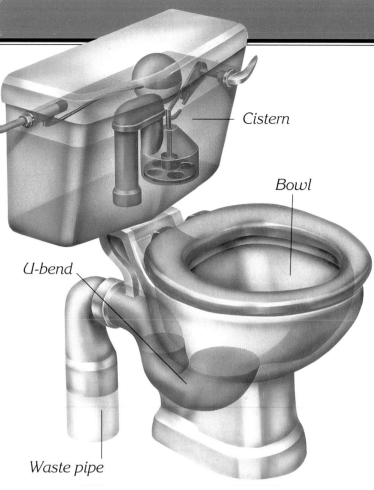

Cistern

Bowl

U-bend

Waste pipe

6. Which tailor's workshop was destroyed because he invented the sewing machine?

Answer: a)

Thimonnier's fellow tailors smashed up his workshop because they thought that his labor-saving invention of 1829 (below) would take work away from them—they were right!

7. Who made the first telescope?

Answer: b)

No one knows exactly who invented the telescope, but Dutch lens-maker Hans Lippershey is usually credited with making the first one, in 1608. Galileo (left) was the first to turn it toward the stars, in 1609.

5. Who designed the flushing toilet?

Answer: a) and b)

Like many inventions, the toilet came about in stages. The Mesopotamians (who lived around 5,000 years ago, in the area now Iraq) had special holed seats with water running beneath to remove waste. The idea was later developed by several English inventors. John Harington published the earliest design for a flushing toilet in 1596—it had goldfish in the cistern! The first practical flushing toilet was made in the 1770s by Alexander Cumming. Then Joseph Bramah added a flap-valve to stop smells rising up from drains. This was replaced by Stephen Green's water-filled U-bend of 1840.

8. When did lawnmowers replace sheep and scythes?

Answer: b)

Many people had tried to make mowers before British inventor Edwin Budding came up with a winning design in 1830.

Budding's hand-pushed lawnmower (1830)

USEFUL WORDS

CIRCUIT *An electric current will flow only if it has a continuous path to follow to and from a supply of electricity. This path is called a circuit. Turning a switch off breaks a circuit. Turning one on, completes it.*

DIESEL ENGINE *Diesel engines are similar to gasoline engines, but in a gasoline engine, the air-fuel mixture is lit by electric sparks from a spark plug. In a diesel engine, the air-fuel mixture is compressed (or squeezed) until it gets so hot that it ignites.*

ELECTRIC MOTOR *A device for converting electrical energy into movement energy. When an electric current is passed through a wire coil inside a magnetic field, the coil rotates.*

ELECTROMAGNET *An electrically produced magnetic field, which can be switched on and off.*

ELECTRONIC *Operated by transistors or microchips.*

GASOLINE ENGINE *An engine in which hot gases are produced by burning gasoline and oxygen gas (from the air). The gases force pistons up and down inside cylinders. Rods and levers change this motion to circular motion, and drive wheels around. (See also page 32.)*

GENERATOR *A machine that changes mechanical energy into electrical energy. British scientist Michael Faraday demonstrated the first generator in 1831, ten years after he had made the first electric motor. Faraday discovered that electricity is produced when a metal disk is spun between the arms of a horseshoe magnet. Later, he found that the same thing happens if a magnet is moved inside a wire coil. The generators that supply most of our electricity today spin wire coils inside giant electromagnets.*

JET ENGINE *An engine in which a jet of hot gases is produced by burning fuel and oxygen (from the air). The gases shoot out of the engine, thrusting the machine into movement.*

LASER *A device that produces a very powerful, narrow beam of light. The first working laser was built by American Theodore Maiman in 1960.*

MAGNETISM *A magnet is an object that attracts some metals (particularly iron) and magnetism is this pulling force. The Earth is a huge natural magnet, with North and South magnetic poles. The needle in a compass is a magnet, which always swings to point* to magnetic North. In the earliest compasses, a kind of iron called lodestone was used as magnetic needle.

MASS-PRODUCTION *Making something in very large quantities, especially using machines.*

MECHANICAL *Operated by a machine (but not electronically).*

MICROCHIP *(Silicon chip or integrated circuit, invented in the late 1950s.) A single tiny chip of material, with all the transistors and wiring needed to make electrical circuits. A $\frac{1}{16}$ square inch microchip in a personal computer may contain one million transistors.*

NUCLEAR REACTION *All substances are made up of invisibly tiny atoms, and the nucleus at the center of each atom contains huge amounts of energy. A nuclear reaction takes place when the nucleus of an atom is changed in some way (usually by splitting it), releasing some of its energy.*

PATENT *A government license granting a person or business the sole right to make and sell something, for a set period of time.*

PROTOTYPE *A first or early version of a machine or device, from which later forms are developed or copied.*

ROCKET *A machine in which thrust comes from burning fuel and oxygen to produce hot gases. Unlike jet engines, rocket engines do not use oxygen from the air and therefore work in space, where there is no air. Rocket engines often use oxygen in liquid form.*

ROTOR *A machine part that moves round and round, such as the blades of a helicopter.*

SATELLITE *Anything that orbits another, much larger, body. Artificial satellites are spacecraft that orbit the Earth.*

STEAM ENGINE *An engine in which steam is produced by burning a fuel (such as coal or wood) to heat water until it boils. The steam drives pistons. In some steam engines, rods and levers change the pistons' back-and-forth or up-down motion to circular motion, driving wheels or gears around.*

TRANSISTOR *A device developed in the late 1940s that is smaller than the thermionic tube and performs the same function in electrical circuits. (See TUBE below, and illustration on page 35.)*

TUBE (THERMIONIC) *Invented in 1904, a device for switching and boosting electric current in electrical circuits. Later largely replaced by transistors. (See illustration on page 35.)*

INDEX